Words that were thought but never spoken

Tyler Letts

Words that were thought but never spoken ©
2022 Tyler Letts

All rights reserved.

No part of this publication may be reproduced, stored in a retrieval system, or transmitted, in any form or by any means, electronic, mechanical, photocopying, recording or otherwise, without the prior written permission of the presenters.

Tyler Letts asserts the moral right to be identified as author of this work.

Presentation by *BookLeaf Publishing*

Web: www.bookleafpub.com

E-mail: info@bookleafpub.com

ISBN : 9789357699648

First edition 2022

DEDICATION

To Allea, a great inspiration and motivation.
To Jake and Andres, thanks for helping me take this chance
To Chloe, thanks for the support

ACKNOWLEDGEMENT

I want to express my special thanks of gratitude to all my lovely readers, fans, friends, family and the wider community, who have always stood by me in my writing journey and have made my dream of becoming a unique author come true. I would also like to thank my late father, who taught me to follow my dreams and never give up no matter how long the road.

Most of all, I want to thank BookLeaf Publishing yet again for giving me the golden opportunity to showcase my talent to the world and publishing my third book!

PREFACE

I have always been passionate about motivating and inspiring others, as it provides me with a real sense of satisfaction. As you read through my poems in this book, you will notice how I keep them sweet, short and simple, without making them overly complex for my audience. This can be challenging at times, but the outcome is always rewarding. I see poetry as a way of escaping from our busy schedules and reflecting on ourselves, so we can come back even stronger. This is very important if we want to learn and succeed in life.

Though I enjoy writing on topics and issues that are currently circulating in the world, as well as from my own personal experiences, I also enjoy writing stimulating pieces to give my audience a glimpse of optimism and reinforcement to make every effort to live life fully and freely. We all need some form of support one way or the other, and I feel that a few Words Of Wisdom can change somebody's life dramatically. I have come across people from all walks of life who have expressed how my words inject their lives with positivity and enthusiasm, which is totally amazing!

Aisha Idris Suleman

Existing

Sometimes I forget to exist
It's not that I stop functioning, it's more like I forget to be me
It's not hard to forget but it's harder to remember
Because I don't want to remember the pains and the sorrows I've felt
But I've forgotten and remembered so much that neither is hard to do anymore
What sweetens the remembering is
The sweet nothings I've come to unconsciously do, the love I've given
The happiness I've experienced and the dreams I've dreamt

Humanity

I enjoy being human
Most people don't because we've done bad things
But I love it because of the love we give each other from time to time
The random conversation you can make with a random stranger
Paying for someone's food
The small greetings to someone we probably won't see again
And that keeps my enjoyment of being human alive
I like humans because they're flawed
And they wholeheartedly accept it
They do try to change
And sometimes they do
But they gain new imperfections
Those imperfections make them interesting
I like humans because their flaws tell stories
And creates the vision of a being that strives for perfection
But may never reach it

Broken

The feeling of not doing what I loved broke me
Specifically not being able to do it broke me
I knew I could but at the same time I couldn't
like there was a door I could walk
to but couldn't open
I tried to open the door but it cracked me
I didn't care so I tried and tried and tried again
The door wouldn't budge until the pain of being
almost broken made itself known
Desperate to open the door I tried once more
only to find myself broken to
pieces
Being broken is never permanent
It's only something temporary under the guise of
permanence
What matters is not that you were broken but
how you put yourself back together
Because the pieces never fit the same
You become the same but different person
Some pieces will be too shattered to be put back
It's hell and it hurts but it is truly impressive and
worst part?
You'll never be the same person
After I rearranged the pieces of myself and built
myself anew
I feared to try the door but I found myself in the
room the door hid

Because as I rebuilt myself the door opened to me
I feared the what the door asked of me but it was amazingly and scarily complex
“Change yourself to become better than you are now
I will break you to be better. Please do become better.”

Indigo

The color of trust and dreams
The color that is deep and sometimes lonely
A color that is deep, inky and sometimes dark
A dark color that brings calming dreams as well as a serene feeling
A color that brings the promise of unbreakable trust
But at times brings the promise of a great loneliness
The closest thing to the to this loneliness is the deep color of the ocean
That brings a calm comforting feeling
The color of a bruise that just sometimes appears over night
The color that shows content but at times the sadness of being unfulfilled
Sadly the world is sometimes is shaded indigo but not the positives or the whole
People who have the shade of indigo
Are trustworthy, calming but feel alone
But this isn't always the case
This is the color that is sometimes shaded alongside blue
This is a color rarely shaded in the face
But the heart and mind
To represent the oddly comforting serene feeling

Blue

The color that everyone says is sad
The color were your happiness can be absent
Sadness and regret is present in its stead
The only color that can't dispersed by the others
The color where tears and sobs seem to be ever present
And in extreme moments depression treads heavily
Everyone denies that they have been shaded in this color
But those shaded in this color can't erase it
It stays longer than the other colors
But the shade can become lighter with the presence of other color
Here's a small piece of advice:
Do what makes you happy
Be around those who make you happy
And Blue will be the lightest color you've been shaded

Violet

The color of uncertainty
That is sweet and beautiful
The color of passion
Where danger is not present
And the clouds of uncertainty are not gray or
white but a deep passionate purple
A passion that is bright but yet dark
A passion bright enough to guide in darkness
But dark enough to blemish the light
A form of passion the rarely harms and produces
beauty
The color of expression
Expression that beautifully feminine
Expression that is soft and kind
And oft forgiving
The color to some, means love
A mix of all the colors on a flag representing
love
A love that has a duality similar to that of yin
and yang or light and dark
That is combined into a beautiful person or
rather color
A color that shades you a deep beautiful color
A shade that is found in passionate and loving
people
Who could have been hurt at some point

A shade that represents being along for the ride
The color that pairs beautifully with indigo
The color that shows joy in uncertainty and that
uncertainty creating passion
The color that helps bring out feminine features
in the soul
The color like flowers that bring peace in
calamity
Flowers with the greatest smell and meaning
The color that helps create a feeling of hope, soft
passion,calming uncertainty
and, for some, love

Orange

A color that signals the start of a new day or new beginning
The shade that shows you've started anew
The shade that starts off the day
The shade that is sometimes felt rather than said
A color that brings warmth and safety
The color that is as warm as a nice ray of sunlight
The color that is like a life vest keeping you afloat
The color that is refreshing and beautiful in a way you know you're safe
A color that helps represent the beauty of the sun and fire
The color that comes in the form of a sunset and sunrise
The color that comes in a flame
This color shows their beauty that is almost never ending
This color also shows the beauty of a friendship
The color where if someone is shaded like this is a friendly,calming,and joyful
A shade that could make someone feel safe in the most dangerous situation
A shade where you are welcome to start again with no shame

This color is perfect representation of warmth,
safety, a new start, joy, and a
beautiful friendship

Yellow

The color of happiness
Happiness that is bright and lights up even the darkest places
The color that makes blue a almost invisible shade
The color of the sunlight that is in the forest
The color of the most beautiful field of sunflowers
The color of undying hope
Hope that could carry anyone through anything
Hope that could win hearts and minds
The color of the stereotype sun
The sun that represents happiness and naïveté
The sun that shines a light on the beauty of the world
A shade where you know a hopeful feeling is bound to follow
A shade where happiness is certain and never far
A color that pairs with blue in with a sense of duality like yin and yang

Green

The color of envy
A color of a wish for what others have
A shade where no one wants to admit that
they've been shaded
A shade of want that is oft unspoken
A color of unkempt want and greed
The color of nature
The shade of beautiful and serene grass
The shade of a calm but wild forest that is not
meant to tampered with
The shade of a field of grass that is meant to be
laid in
The color of positivity
A shade of positive feelings and actions that are
hardly rewarded
A shade of doing good things with no cause
The color of good intentions
The shade that is beloved in the right context
A color that is most times believed to be shaded
lightly to hide another color
This color shows a unpleasant envy,the beauty
of nature,and a kind positivity
All of which pierces the soul in many ways

Red

The color of anger and unbridled rage
A shade of a unclear mind
A shade that shows that you've been pushed a bit too hard
A shade that matches an inferno that is uncontrollable
The color of undeniable beauty
The shade of a woman who looks good for herself and the occasional date
The shade of a dress that will stay in the memories of many
The shade of woman who states what she wants with a look
The color of danger
A shade telling you to turn back
A shade that cautions you to stay back
A shade that signals a burn or intense pain
The color of a burning passion
The shade of a passion that shows you will stop at nothing to achieve your goal

Grey

Grey
A color often mistaken for its metallic cousin, silver
But unlike its cousin it has almost no meaning other than true balance
The world is painted this color even more so than indigo
Most people see the world as grey's parent colors
Black and White
Not to say there aren't spots of black or white but there are more so shades of
dark and light
Not to say balance is grey's only meaning
It can also mean knowledge
It shades scholars and philosophical learners to represent what the knowledge
could be used for
It shades those who do destroy to build
It shades people who work in the dark to serve the light
It covers those who see nothing as wrong or right but leave it to perspective
It paints the mind and soaks the soul
I believe grey is a color best left to perspective
Because it can be seen as beautiful by some

Or terrifyingly unknown like space or the sea
But much like both you could search to find
what is in it and give it meaning
Or leave it be
Because it strips you of all your dreams and
fears leaving you unbearably bare

Inside My Head

I hate being inside my own head
Inside my head the world is loud because as a child I was forced to be quiet
So I said what I wanted to say in my head as a yell
But my screams and yells were heard by no one
I hated being inside my head because it always felt like a padded soundproof
room
I felt trapped in that room for years
But the door has been opened and I can hear myself yelling
I don't mean to yell, I just feel like I'm inside my head again

One More

One more.
It's all I ask for of almost anything
One more hug, because your embrace comforts
me, makes me feel safe and
eases my soul
One more smile, because it's a beautiful thing to
see
One more kiss, only because their soft and sweet
One more minute, because I wanna spend more
time with you, even if it is a
small amount
One more hour, because I never have enough
time to write, say or do the right
things I need to do
One more day for me to love you and you to me
because I want to feel loved for
just a day longer but more than that I want to
make you feel loved just a day
more
One more month for the memories I want to
make while I'm still a young carefree
kid
One more year, just so I can make things right
with the people I love and myself
But I guess asking for one more makes me
greedy and I know the less I have of

something is the more I love and appreciate them

My Words Have No Meaning

My words have little meaning to those who hear
them
Because I speak with little knowledge or
experience
I haven't lived life to where I could give
knowledge or advice to others that would
be useful
Words value shouldn't be based on one's
experience or knowledge
But to others words could mean the world and
become a bond to the soul
But for some, words mean nothing and actions
mean everything
Words could be a bond and send a message
But actions will send a message, no matter how
it is interpreted, rarely and only
rarely will they become bond.
Both my actions and my words send neither
They hold no meaning to no one because I speak
too much and act too little
But to a few my words and actions form a bond
and send a message
Those are the few I trust and believe
But to others my words hold not a ounce of
meaning or my actions worth less
than a pound

I'm a Mess

I'm a mess, so why do you deny that you're fed up?
I'm a mess that hinders your progress and I hate it
Because there's so much more you can do without me
Why do you think that I'm your mess to clean up?
Its painful to see to see you crumble as I mess up
I'm a mess that holds you too close
Or you choose to stay, how would I know the difference?
But you're cleaning me up anyway
I'm doing better because you help
Yeah, I'm still a mess but a mess that's getting cleaned up
There's so much you have done with me
You've progressed so far, even while cleaning me up
I've always been your mess, wether I wanted to be or not
You crumbled so you could clean up with the pieces and put yourself back
together
I didn't hold you close but you choose to stay close because you didn't want me

to be alone

Depression Part 1

I've never felt this way and I'm not sure how I
should feel
The world says that I should feel sad and tired
all the time
I do but it's become easier to hide it than show
others
I've never wanted this
With people asking me what caused it but I'm
not sure where it came from
And during the night by myself sadness washes
over like a flood and tears come
like rain
I'm told that it's not normal to feel like this
Then what should I feel
Cause now I feel like I'm digging my own grave
and like I'm gonna go into it
early
But I don't wanna die, I just wanna Stop
Existing

Sadness

A grey cloudy emotion that is felt by all
My mind hates feeling sad but stays sad because
it can find no reason to leave
that state
The world bears with this emotion but tells
people to stop feeling it
People judge how sad you should be by what
your life is
With out knowing what caused that sadness
But sadness isn’t always an uninvited guest
But instead an a lack of happiness

Depression Part 2

My emotions feel like the blood got cut off to
my leg, I feel Nothing but then when
the blood comes back I feel Everything
But in spite of that wake up and put a smile on
my face because I want no one to
know horrible I really feel
As much as I feel numb I can only find one way
to describe it as having a void
that any emotion can fill
My Heart hurts and I don't know how to feel I
just wanna sleep all day and not
come out but I don't wanna live like this
I wanna stay in the dark as much as I wanna see
the light
Every time I try and go towards the light I just
get dragged down by my demons
and painful thoughts
But there's always someone who will try and
help me into the light

Depression Part 3

Alone.
That's what I think I am
I've felt alone for so long but why
But there is hardly ever a reason it just happens
Sometimes it's not just feeling alone sadly when
I do I choose to be alone and
listen to sad music and make it worse
I stay quiet and anxiety teams up with my
depression making me wanna scream
and shout
But not in happiness but in pain
Never the physical kind of pain, but the I don't
know what I'm fucking doing
mental pain
The pain where crawling and crying in a corner
seems like the only fucking
option
But sadly I can't fucking cry, I don't wanna cry
in front of the wrong people
Or look in the mirror and see a fucking
disappointment and cry harder
The question everyone asks is would your
younger self be proud of you?
My answer has become no, he fucking wouldn't
and if I could give my past self
advice

Do what makes you happy, choose the option
that will get you emotionally
developed but not in the shit way
But that gets you experiences and memories
Please love yourself and for the love of God stop
overthinking
Cause I can’t stop doing it

Insecure

I'm sorry if ask if you care so much
It's just sometimes I think you don't
And if you don't answer I'll think too much and make my own
Such as 'I'm never enough' or 'I'm not worth the effort'
Sometimes I'm scared that you'll just replace me
I'm scared I'm just a late night talk for your convenience
And sometimes I think the words you say are never true and are only said so I
leave you alone
Please don't think I'm weird, it's just that words mean so much to me
Your words mean a lot to me, when I know they shouldn't
I'm sorry, I just haven't been validated most of my life
'I'm proud of you' isn't apart of my family's dialogue options
'You did great' weren't words I heard too often
And my family only calls me out on my downfalls
I'm always the back end of a joke in a group of friends

So when I’m surprised at any compliments you give
Please understand.

Allea

A walking ray of sunshine and beauty wrapped
inside of a human body
If she controlled the weather it probably be
sunny with some clouds to keep the
sun out her eyes
She's calmly energetic
Wildly focused
Far kinder than I believe humanly possible
Her brain is scarily and amazingly beautiful and
wondrously creative
Her eyes shine just a tad bit brighter than the sun
She sounds busy but somehow she finds time for
the sun to shine right on her
Her mind moves so fast it gives light
competition
She's amazing in some simple but complex way

www.ingramcontent.com/pod-product-compliance
Lightning Source LLC
LaVergne TN
LVHW020532160826
845677LV00015B/4010

* 9 7 8 9 3 5 7 6 9 9 6 4 8 *